DON'T ARM WRESTLE A PIRATE

DON'T ARM WRESTLE A PIRATE

101 REALLY BAD IDEAS

WORDS BY DAVE SKINNER AND HENRY PAKER
DRAWINGS BY HENRY PAKER

HODDER &
STOUGHTON

First published in Great Britain in 2007 by Hodder & Stoughton

An Hachette Livre UK company

1

Copyright © Dave Skinner and Henry Paker 2007

The right of Dave Skinner and Henry Paker to be identified as the Authors of the Work has been asserted by them in accordance with the Copyright, Designs and Patents Act 1988.

A CIP catalogue record for this title is available from the British Library

ISBN 978 0 340 95105 7
Trade Paperback ISBN 978 0 340 95106 4

Printed and bound by L.E.G.O. SpA, Vicenza, Italy

Hodder & Stoughton policy is to use papers that are natural, renewable and recyclable products and made from wood grown in sustainable forests. The logging and manufacturing processes are expected to conform to the environmental regulations of the country of origin.

Hodder & Stoughton Ltd
338 Euston Road
London NW1 3BH

www.hodder.co.uk

With thanks to:

Geoff and Inez Skinner,
Yakup and Ruth Paker,
Alice O'Hanlon,
Nick Davies,
Camilla Hornby
and all at Hodder and Stoughton

1 Don't remove nasal hair with pliers

2 Don't trust anyone with a pixellated face

3 Don't forget your flag

4 Don't catch a fridge

5 Don't sell your face
as advertising space

6 Don't advertise your PIN number to strangers

7

Don't bring your
kid to work

8 Don't go into the woods dressed as a giant acorn

9 Don't brush against a footballer

10 Don't assume all employers have a dress-down Friday policy

11 Don't borrow things without asking

12 Don't replace something you've lost with a cheap copy

13 Don't assume all wardrobes lead to Narnia

14 Don't remove a stray eyelash with a vacuum cleaner

15 Don't smuggle your
pet on holiday

16 Don't 'go large' at the cinema

17 Don't play Sudoku on Acid

18 Don't arm wrestle a pirate

19 Don't assume you'll never find love

20 Don't run away to join the flea circus

21 Don't trust your cat

22 Seriously, don't trust your cat

23 Don't play
Nut Allergy Roulette

24 Don't wear the same outfit as the bride

25 Don't challenge a witch to a game of Paper, Scissors, Stone

26 Don't share a flat with your arch nemesis

27 Don't let a child design your tattoo

28 Don't greet a stranger the way your dog does

29 Don't go bowling with zombies

30 Don't hire your own disciples

31 Don't stalk your own wife

32 Don't go on holiday with your arch nemesis

33 Don't let super models cater your wedding

34 Don't visit your granny dressed as the Grim Reaper

35 Don't rely on a mime
artist in an emergency

36 Don't lock The A-Team in your delicatessen

37 Don't go wakeboarding

38 Don't wait until you're 80 to streak at Wimbledon

39 Don't rely on two mime artists in an emergency

40 Don't let your nephew ride your dog

41 Don't ask a dwarf if he's lost his mummy and daddy

42 Don't buy a back wig

43 Don't hire a troupe of mime artists to help you move house

44 Don't build a 'sexy' snowman

45 Don't over deoderise

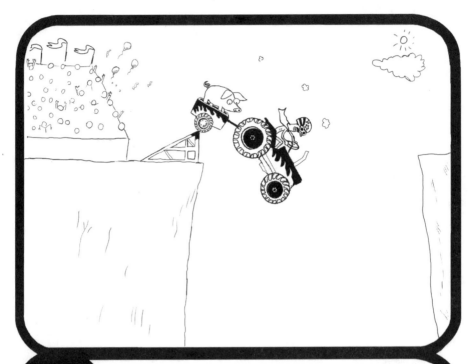

46 Don't try to jump the Grand Canyon on a tractor

47 Don't build your own i-pod

48 Don't go grouse shooting
dressed as a giant grouse

49 Don't propose with Powerpoint

50 Don't give your nephew a "Birthday surprise he'll never forget"

51 Don't worship an effigy of your flatmate

52 Don't let cowboys build your extension

53 Don't date David Blaine

54 Don't sub-contract out your babysitting job

55 Don't boast about the size of your poos

56 Don't try to force your way into the Matrix

57 Don't floss with cheese wire

58 Don't kiss David Blaine
goodnight

59 Don't hide inside a tiger

60 Don't build an elaborate machine that could accidentally hurl you into the white hot heart of the sun

61 Don't interrupt someone's
last words

62 Don't offer marriage guidance to mormons

63 Don't go into your parents'
room without knocking

64 Don't over-react

65 Don't give a balloon to a supermodel

66 Don't try to steal the limelight at the school nativity

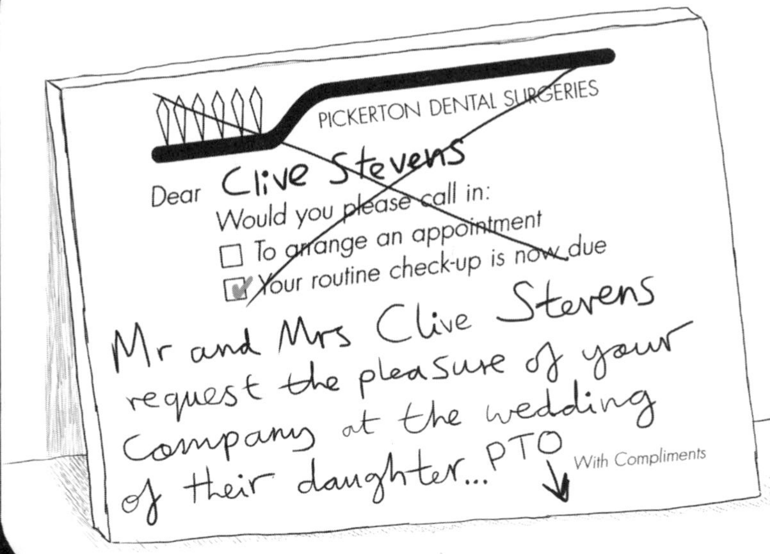

67 Don't be a cheapskate

68 Don't attempt to harness the power of eccentricity

69 Don't buy a dog that looks like you

10 Don't high-five an ant

71 Don't cheat at the Olympics

72 Don't run at scissors

73 Don't count on Wasp Man

74 Don't pick a favourite child

75 Don't badger a badger

76 Don't kid yourself

77 Don't get a nose job from a surrealist plastic surgeon

78 Seriously, don't badger a badger

79 Don't tell your children about the futility of life

80 Don't compensate for baldness by cultivating other hair

81 Don't throw a stick
near a guide dog

82 Don't eat cheese at night

83 Don't hire
Boozy The Clown

84 Don't wash your clothes with you still in them

85 Don't jump out of a plane with a watermelon strapped to your back

86 Don't go too retro

87 Don't trust the internet

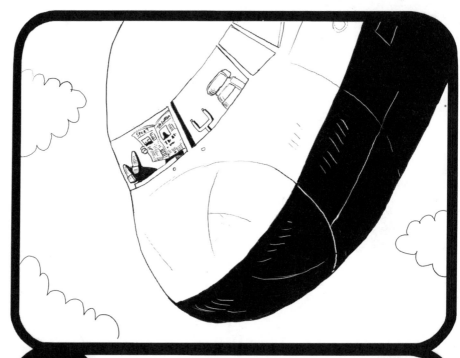

88 Don't make your imaginary friend your co-pilot

89 Don't "Say it with stubble"

90 Don't assume all koalas
are cute and cuddly

91 Don't let Damien Hirst look after your granny for the afternoon

92 Don't play with glue

93 Don't visit space with a budget airline

94 Don't drink and knit

95 Don't disguise a bald
spot with chocolate spread

96 Don't climb a Bonsai tree

97 Don't give up breathing for lent

98 Don't give bees for Christmas

99 Don't assume everybody shares your interests

100 Don't try drawing left-handed for a change

101 Don't expect a happy ending